Gateshead Council

Due for Return	Due for Return	Due for Return
		2 5 SEP 2019
		2 2 DEC 2021
		4 MAY 2022
	9 - AUG 2017	
1 9 NOV 2010	- 7 MAY 2019	2 3 AUG 2023
- 6 SEP 2012	2 0 FEB 2020	
3 1 MAY 2014		1 4 SEP 2023
- 4 NOV 2014	1 4 JUL 2021	4 JAN 2024
2 3 FEB 2016	1 4 NOV 2023	1 1 AUG 2025

Visit us at:

www.gateshead.gov.uk/books

Tel: 0191 433 8400

C1 691187 60 3D

Bugs that make food

Bee Menu

the BIG PICTURE

Louise Spilsbury

Published 2010 by
A&C Black Publishers Ltd.
36 Soho Square, London, W1D 3QY

www.acblack.com

ISBN HB 978-1-4081-2788-9
     PB 978-1-4081-3164-0

Text copyright © 2010 Louise Spilsbury

The right of Louise Spilsbury to be identified as the author of this work has been asserted by her in accordance with the Copyrights, Designs and Patents Act 1988.

A CIP catalogue for this book is available from the British Library.

All rights reserved. No part of this publication may be reproduced in any form or by any means – graphic, electronic or mechanical, including photocopying, recording, taping or information storage and retrieval systems – without the prior permission in writing of the publishers.

Every effort has been made to trace copyright holders and to obtain their permission for use of copyright material. The author and publishers would be pleased to rectify any error or omission in future editions.

This book is produced using paper that is made from wood grown in managed, sustainable forests. It is natural, renewable and recyclable. The logging and manufacturing processes conform to the environmental regulations of the country of origin.

Produced for A&C Black by Calcium. www.calciumcreative.co.uk

Printed and bound in China by C&C Offset Printing Co.

All the internet addresses given in this book were correct at the time of going to press. The author and publishers regret any inconvenience caused if addresses have changed or sites have ceased to exist, but can accept no responsibility for any such changes.

Acknowledgements

The publishers would like to thank the following for their kind permission to reproduce their photographs:

Cover: Shutterstock: Tischenko Irina (front), Alle (back). **Pages:** Shutterstock: Takiev Alexander 23, Alle 15, Anyka 11, Ason 6–7, Nikola Bilic 14, Katrina Brown 8, 16, Chas 13, Steve Cukrov 7, Nikolay Stefanov Dimitrov 16–17, Dimos 22–23, Tomo Jesenicnik 10, Kirsanov 17, Joanna Zopoth-Lipiejko 3, Manfredxy 4–5, Dave Massey 2–3, Zacarias Pereira da Mata 1, MilousSK 12, Fedorov Oleksiy 8–9, 14–15, Photoslb.com 9, Pixinity 12–13, Marianna Raszkowska 20–21, Vladimir Sazonov 4–5, Bruce T. Smith 18–19, Suravid 10–11, Filipe B. Varela 24, Kulish Viktoria 19, WDG Photo 18, Yaroslav 21.

Contents

Honey Menu 4
Honeybee Homes 6
Inside a Nest 8
Teamwork 10
Honey Recipe 12
Making Honey 14
Honey For Us 16
Different Honey 18
Brilliant Bees 20
Glossary 22
Further Reading 23
Index 24

Honey Menu

Bees are amazing. They make honey that they can eat, and we can eat it too!

Honeybees

There are many kinds of bee, but honeybees make the most honey. They live all over the world.

Bees make honey to eat in winter.

Don't touch!

Bees look beautiful, but beware! The yellow and black stripes on their body are a warning. If you touch a bee, it might sting you.

Hands off!

Honeybee Homes

Honeybees live together in nests. **Some nests are small, but some are very big.**

Making nests

Bees make nests in all sorts of places. They make nests on trees and bushes, in caves, and on cliffs.

Home sweet home

Busy bees

Nests are busy places! Bees make and store all their honey in their nests.

This bees' nest hangs from a tree.

Inside a Nest

Inside a honeybees' nest there are many little cells. These are like tiny rooms where young bees live and honey is stored.

Same shape, same size

The cells are all the same shape and size. Each cell has six sides, so they fit together neatly to form a **honeycomb**.

I'm buzzy working!

Wax works

Bees make cells from **wax**. To make wax, bees mix **fat** from their stomachs with spit from their mouths.

Bees take away dirt, poo and old food to keep the nest clean.

Teamwork

Bees in a nest work as a team. Different bees do different jobs.

Queen in charge!

The queen bee lays the eggs. Male bees called drones **mate** with the queen so she can lay eggs. Worker bees collect and make food. They also care for the eggs and young bees.

Every bee has a job to do.

Killer bees

Killer bees make a lot of honey, but hundreds of them attack at once if their nest is in danger!

Buzz off!

Honey Recipe

Honeybees need nectar to make honey. Nectar is a sweet juice found in flowers.

Busy bees

Worker honeybees suck up the nectar through their tongues. They carry the nectar back to the nest in a special part of their body.

A bee uses its tongue like a drinking straw!

Dance with me!

Honeybees tell each other where to find flowers by dancing! They walk in a wiggly line to show other bees which way to go.

This way!

Making Honey

Worker bees feed some nectar to the bees that stay behind in the nest. They use the rest of the nectar to make honey.

Spit and mix!

Honeybees mix nectar with juices in their mouths. They put drops of this mixture into the honeycomb cells. They fan it with their wings to dry it.

Runny honey!

Honey is the sticky mixture bees put inside cells.

Honey stores

In winter, the flowers on most plants die. Without flowers, there is no nectar for bees to make honey. Bees put wax lids on honey cells to keep their honey fresh.

Honey For Us

We get our honey from beehives. These are nests that beekeepers **build for bees to make honey in.**

Enough for bees, too

When honey in a hive is ready, beekeepers lift out the honeycombs. They scrape the wax lids off the cells and take out the honey. They then put it in jars.

Oi!

Take care!

Bees get angry if people touch their nest. This is why beekeepers wear clothes and hats that cover their body and face.

This honeycomb is full of honey.

Different Honey

The taste and smell of a honey depends on the kind of flowers the nectar came from.

Honey flavours

Eucalyptus trees grow mainly in Australia, so that is where most eucalyptus honey comes from. Heather grows well in Scotland, so that is where most heather-flavoured honey comes from.

Sunflower honey from France is thick and yellow!

Honey time

In warm places such as Africa, there are flowers all year round. This means bees make honey here for most of the year.

Brilliant Bees

Bees are brilliant. As well as making honey that we can eat, they help plants to grow!

Bee gardeners!

When a bee visits a flower, it rubs its body against the **pollen** on the flower. When the bee lands on another flower, some of this pollen rubs onto the new flower. Pollen helps the new flower make **seeds**. New plants can grow from the seeds.

Help!

A bee may visit 100 flowers in just one trip!

Bees in trouble

Some bees are dying because people are cutting down trees, so there are fewer places for bee nests.

Pollen

Glossary

beekeepers people who keep hives of bees

fat thick substance stored in an animal's body

honeycomb set or group of six-sided cells that bees build from wax

mate something animals do to make babies

nectar sweet, sugary substance found in the centre of a flower's petals

nest place an animal builds to live in

pollen powder from a flower that can make other flowers grow seeds

seeds seeds are made inside flowers. Seeds can grow into new plants.

wax stuff that bees make in their bodies. Bees use wax to make the cells in a honeycomb.

Further Reading

Websites

Find out more about honey and bees at:
www.honey.com

Discover more about bees at:
animals.nationalgeographic.com/animals/bugs/honeybee.html

Books

Honey Bees (Blastoff! Readers: World of Insects) by Colleen Sexton, Children's Press (2007).

Honey (Food) by Louise Spilsbury, Heinemann (2001).

How Bees Make Honey (Rainbows Nature) by Helena Ramsey, Evans Brothers Ltd (2005).

Index

beehives 16
beekeepers 16–17

cells 8–9, 16

fat 9
flavours of honey 18
flowers 12, 15, 18, 19, 20

honey 4, 7, 11, 12, 14, 15, 16–17, 18–19
honey stores 15
honeybees 4, 8, 12–13, 14
honeycomb 8, 14, 16, 17

killer bees 11

mate 10

nectar 12, 14, 15, 18
nests 6–7, 11, 12, 16, 17, 21

pollen 20

queen bee 10

seeds 20
sting 4
stripes 4

wax 9, 15, 16
worker bees 10, 12, 14